t

MW01231901

for Louise

and in memory of my mother

Also by Anthony Joseph:

DESAFINADO

First published in 1997

1 3 5 7 9 10 8 6 4 2

Anthony Joseph © 1997

Anthony Joseph has asserted his right under
the Copyright and Patents Act, 1988
to be identified as the author of this work.

First published in the United Kingdom 1997
by Poisonenginepress, 31 Leconfield House,
Champion Hill, London SE5 8AY

A CIP catalogue record for this book
is available from the British Library

Typeset by Nia Roberts

ISBN 0 9524152 1 6

teragaton

Anthony Joseph

poisonenginepress

CONTENTS

4 TERAGATONIC SAMPLING

PREFACE

Un portrait symbolique d'elle et moi
a symbolic portrait of her and I[1]

Recounting to me a recent dream, the poet speaks of a certain elevation from which he at that moment she, this woman suspended in an elevated house- a floating aeola of sorts. She jumps from the deck of this house, to escape into a pail of water. That is, she jumps from the house to the ground below-our foreground of the whole action-sequence[2] -only then to emerge out of this minimalist arrangement of pail and water in the greatest of swathes. And when this character, who he first sees as distanced from himself emerges, she *turns into*/becomes him,[3] running, resuming the escape.[4] This morphemic technology is pervasive througout the text-it is both technological and personal.

> the way i ran tho' that i might die.the way i ran i
> ran sideways fastest, tried runnin front out bt run
> same ol'can't run dream sequence

-running&can't[5]

---

[1]this title, elliptical and definitely somnambulist is in reference to an imaginary drawing Andre Breton does of he and the recurring protaganist of his own dream text(and life)- Nadja

[2]with regards to further notion of action-sequence see section two - Hicona.

[3]see also Indian Red- the actor's my father unmasked as myself at his age...

[4]the emergence of the entire form of this being soon to transform is overwhelming. If one can see this woman jumping from the deck of the house into a bucket then emerging, this series of movements has a certain quality of overwhelming proportions. If one were to film it, the close-up would be preferred. There would be an immediacy of contact between her and the viewer. Throughout the text we are treated to the frightening prospects of such views.

If we live in a time of uncertainty, of what is felt to be the end and loss of a discernible way forward, of what can be simply summarized as 'endgame' theories. What then can such an insistence on the autonomy of art represent but at the very least the possibility of a way out, running rampant to the precipes we approach. Your reading cannot be otherwise. Let the text take you - do not let it breathe - witness its characters, its narrative as a possibility in a world which says otherwise.

Our poet speaks frankly of this loss, the core object lost in simulacra, he says, and feels and is at most times caught in its sticky film of deceit. What he offers us are its visceral terrors. Anthony Joseph assaults this lethargy of an easy sense of displacement (from country or otherwise[6]). He offers us another or rather proffers to offer another possibility to/of what has become popular and acceptable as the protracted preachings of an apocalyptic nature known as post modernity. Like this woman in the dream -emerging then resuming her/his escape-there is a suggestion of forwardness even in the midst of the degradation we know and feel as late capitalism. Please witness what would seem elliptical is in fact a set of attempts to literal/ly catch us in our descent.

---

[5]In the absurdity of the situations he describes as dream-action sequences, the absurdity becomes all the more bearable in seeing it as a series of sequences. As he says, if it can be seen it can be filmed.

[6]see for example, Plasticine in section one- OldIron&BrokeDickNeoljisms

...they come
runnincarryin
her in their arms
i open the door-rush-for her head to support
a man rides past on a flamingo

-untitled (from Oldiron&brokedicknelojisms)

What is present in Anthony Joseph's text is a reconstitutive aesthetic, an aesthetic of reconstituting yields, effects and possibilities and not just the simplicity of open transparence philosopher Jean Baudrillard exhorts. He offers us the impossibility of possibility rather than its own impossibility. Even the brief characters and episodes of this semi-narrative spew it back in deposits of poetic retention. And as you discover when reading the text, repetitive images, similar screams and continuous cries indicate a narrative, at the very least, of the imagination. It is I would say, to appropriate Andre Breton's phrase – an imaginary portrait of her and I. Her saving, our saving . To enter deep into the precipes of this text is to enter into a certain semblance, at the very least, of emerging.

Anthony Joseph enters us into speed. He cannot go back.[7] He can only look forward and in this uncertainty of looking is the necessity of transparency. He offers us a vista rather than a view. We are led neither back nor to a similar moment of stasis. Neither are we told to wait, we are not waiting for something-it has passed ; if it comes

---

[7]He can only glean its episodes as resources of forward movement-living for the next second. Are we not all in this permanence of fast forward. Some denying, others trying in vain to glean slowness in speed.

back, its initial suprise will take on a certain banality.
Speed. A moment of indecision -to query a phrase-in
that moment you may miss something. He refuses the
false judgements of return. Instead you are offered a
glimpse of the liminal and its bent skeleton deformities.

The poet however, appears unaware of the pervasity of a
transformative character throughout his poesis but she
continually rares her head throughout the text. Who is
this woman? The her in their arms, the undeniable
dramatis personae which repeats itself each time, masked
differently, masked/unmasked ? I am not sure. This is not
a deconstruction but a reading. Are these characters part
some larger constellation of idols who cannot go back?
There is in here, in his constellation of recurring
personae, the metaphysics of another world-or rather a
world within the absurdity of this one - a parallel
present. He calls this place Teragaton. Enter Teragaton,
have the courage.

head down walking street such sadness
so went to the DoctorPsychiatristPsychoanalyst
-light blowing tru curtains in the room-talkin right&camomile
bt eventually filld wt much pain
i break and lay my head on her breast

-matrixs

JAMES OSCAR
New York City

INTRODUCTION

to name something is to wait for it in the place
you think it will pass
AMIRI BARAKA

Teragaton is a place I arrived at. To arrive I made
departures from sense, syntax-logic, conscious focus,
preset matrices into an explosion/implosion of raw word
and solid thought matter - a bulk of chaos containing
the pre-selective text.

This place has been called different names:

the Unconsciousubconscious
the Surreal
No-mind
the Dream
Zen
Funk
Doors of perception
Conceptualism
Jazz
Madness

I call it core. *Teragaton*.

To locate it I had to locate myself in a parallel present,
unravel my tongue, reclaim all headspace, disengage
critical analysis - to find the core object lost in
Simulacra, until the text becomes a mind-map and if
possible, a trans-literation before it is censored by
consciousness.

Essentially, I had to write until I wrote without writing, accessing the unconscious by using its language.

writing is a physical act.
or...even the position of the body affects the way you write

Constant becomes *natural*, like blood. The physical act of writing only its transfusion.

why
because we are experiencing a crisis of representation –
conceptual colonialism.

how
*by being a **transparent mirror:** absorbing and reflecting at the same time*
automatic/trance/stream of un&con/writing with eyes closed/ambidextrous writing/writing during the dream/then on waking while conscious is still asleep/writing irretrievable text to escape the ego/teragatonic sampling of written matter /blackwadadamambos/ 'cess'/et.cetera
some traditional methods were also used.

The unconscious gathers. Then the conscious selects. Teragaton is situated at their intersection, where words are used *not necessarily to communicate an idea but as tools to plant a wordless truth.*

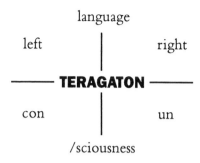

CUBISTEPISTEMOLOGY

The brain could be seen as a library from which we choose meaning so unconsciously that perception becomes a habit. For example, the scent of a flower is received by the nose which then transmits the relevant information to the brain. The brain then provides its perception. But why not let the scent describe itself?

THE ARROGANCE OF NAMING

or we name things so that we can control them

Book is ink and paper .Becomes *text* only when read/ *charged* with *meaning* by the reader.
But when I turn away is it still a book, am I sure, is it still there, which dimension does it occupy in the absence of light? If it becomes a book only when we perceive and name it, maybe then it ceases to exist at all and becomes a simulation.

POSTCOLONIALINGUISTICS&PHONETICFUNK

Kamau Brathwaite's metaphor: the Caribbean as a stone thrown from Africa; each time it skims the water-an island.

My English is not native or natural. It's one language to replace another that's been lost, forgotten or rinsed. The closest approximation of the original I have is the one spoken in the Caribbean with original African wordbeat.

talking drum not morse code
    meaning manipulates sound manipulates meaning
        an'form is what happens

OLDIRON&BROKEDICKNEOLOJISMS

uncle martin mechanic said so.he jus'love ol'iron.fixin buses.nuts and spanners, screws and their drivers-I do with letters

...as slick as a brokedick dog
MILES DAVIS

26 letters are not enough to swallow neolojisms of syntax between gaps in language barriers

EUROPEISINMYASS

hypnotic letters instigate mindstate for access to Teragatonic pleasures

When I came to London in 1989 I realised, that in order to adapt to the city with my sanity intact, certain adjustments would have to be made. If not I would be re-colonized. The resistance is stronger than memory but **europeisinmyass.** relentlessly. The text represents a hyperspacial discourse in which Euromericafricaribbean agents all have offices in the belly of this beast.

HICONA *or pimp funk ina-jimmypump*

a dream is really a text

If it can be seen it can be filmed. Then this is a scene by scene treatment of 20 images captured on Teragatonic film: written during the dream then exposed in a jimmypump.

TERAGATONIC SAMPLING
Of written matter. A Collage of notes, quotes, found text, dialogue and assorted experiments with tone and linguistic muscle.

Note:
This text consists, for the most part,of experiments. The reader is therefore not its audiance but a participant in the expericncc.

ANTHONY JOSEPH

Conscious discourse is rather like those manuscripts
where a first text has been rubbed out and covered
by a second. In such manuscripts the first text can
be glimpsed through the gaps in the second. The true
speech - the unconscious - breaks through usually in a
veiled and incomprehensible form.

MADAN SARUP

1
oldiron&brokedickneolojisms

BLAKDADAMASONSONG

for ted joans

mo`bone than gravediggerboots!
i eclipsed doped scopednscooped wt open palm
turnd to face the surf-
        surface of the moon

i came from blood wept rain an come
swallowd entire oceans whole
carri/d m`muscle`n
russian armyhat warm
        wt blaksurrealistmanifesto btween elbows

       i sharpnd my toes
got deep suck sippin hot.orange juice in Gaza
red&wideeyed sniffin snaildung in Accra

my tongue super my tong/bcome:
      spittin:
      OBEAH MANTRAS

lizard tippd spear tru
all cold froze rainbows you
   swallowd me whole you
      suckd me dry

CAMEL, A SMALL PAINTING

camel a small painting,the so called "white lady"
(opposite) the Tiv are renowned as thatchers, Blier
1987- a veritable hypocaust. Akua ba.it has been-
fanti doll clearly suspended frm his neck, or
libel.140.141 wooden-terracotta, Nok culture-
bronze-clearly defined. infantile although
the face is bearded. fetish lids, an imported mirror-
the fewer-the lid,himself-the lids vary in
complexity. some sculptures are kept wrapped-the
fierce body.we removed its garments-fetish
figure, nine days later to be burned-small pox-
african mask-monoxylous, ie. to represent water-
out of a single block of wood-mask of identical
appearance. BaYaKa eyes and the elbows on knees-
mythical creatures-oBo EKiti,
Cassava, Lobi-modern place names-woman
holding a fan (now bent) Rubin-ht.45½ in.oron.L.
8½ in.camel,a small painting

THE JAZZ CRUSADERS LIVE IN * NEW YORK *

i looked tru my 509 albums fo`Jazz
skimmin brimmin
sweet Jazz
street Jazz
sparklin Jazz
ripplin Jazz
bt i was low
              on jazz an`
Ramsey Lewis wont do
create that late
friday night
alone bt for
Jazz Coltrane dear old
Stockholm
one down one up

blow!

even Oscar Peterson wont blend wt these orange walls

i wanted to
get in touch
with strong prose i chose
`roi jones:**blackmagicpoems**
`cause tonite.tonite is no
Capt.Beefheart.not tonite is no
Chick Corea.not tonite is no
Canned Heat.no.tonite is no
tonight is

sardine a la carte`n
ornettedextergordonduke
Ellington
no blues jus`Jazz
skimmin brimmin 52nd
streetJazz sweetJazz
sparklin niggaskin ripplin Jazz

no blues
no blues
no more blues

gas shines the asphalt
vapoursburn nostrilhair
i blow
the horn twice
as a lizard skidsacross
d'slicksmoothchromebonnetsheen.they come
runnincarryin
her in their arms
i open the door-rush-for her head to support
a man rides past on a flamingo

MR. HENRY

doors are late for nectie dancers-
sharp tongue cuts mine-swish-
my bone dry cumshot splashes-
shatters in inner-living aftershock-
whips the rim wt-
KANANGA WATER

shht.we bn bustd-go get de pliers
de police comin
i nevr bn caugt bfor

stones rattlin in palmcup –
sunday tied wt palm-
pressure gauge pumps pure gush-
rotates!splendid!my boot kicks vision-
of the of the of the eyes of the-
yellow eyes of the transparent face-
peeping tru dawn

WILDLIFE
for james oscar

1
cafe.the living room.soho 9.30.
we are words writing themselves
our lips move like pens extend as fingers-
(text&con.text.)
`form is what happens`

Bateman st.Rasa Sayang.loreli.
breath–fire–air
most abundant always more-
(affect & effect.)
pause.another cigarette.

2
a piano seduces a memory
waves&sand crash against stone
(ero or corosion)

The Thunderstone: *my grandmother believed
these fell from the sky.they did.
                    i realised years later they were
                                    meteorite particles.*

Testing the Thunderstone:
*tie wt thread the smooth black stone found in the
                sungreen savannah.
            allow to hang-a pendulum
                stab wt fire-
            the stone should not fall*

a scorpion in a crease of brown pine.
burn between scissors then eat limbxlimb
(antidote against its sting)

an iguana in our backyard.
when we killd it we found
eggs in her stomach

FAKEDADAPOEM

psychological strangling not 39
16yr **Excuses No** Sylvester
neighbour condemned to old had
jury south been defence injection
problems a mentally 1976 objections
in the Carolina was that had yesterday
despite told by him was in which lethal
aged Adams executed retarded death
and for he

TINCTURE

a red sun the size of belmont rises over jerningham avenue
its rays are webs are ladders to every street here
the red
bronze/
steelpansticksonfire-gold
smell of fresh paint
on the midnight robbers collection box

khakibootsblew frm 2nd avenue

tincture

bright orangegreen
with the red of hibiscus scent
over the blacktonguewoman fence
& her beardeddaughter their
windows tied wit steel

the sun risen also rises here frm it down one of its
ladders

a figure appears

MATRIXS

head down walking street such sadness so
went to the DoctorPsychiatristPsychoanalyst
-light blowing tru curtains in the room-talkin right&camomile
bt eventually filld wt much pain
i break an`lay my head on her breast

when day broke him frm his sweatsleep.or the optical
illusions of the night before.hs hands shook himself
aware of the mirror repeating infinity wt
intense precision-this void in mandrake-
parahanthesis.these beasts.he confided in the paraffin
night he could find it there-
in the village.green mouths obscured by matrixs

wt this movement when i write i'm aware of this also to
capture motion outside of a timeframe-
bt in an almost existentialist way the sublime can be accessed
by
hyperplane interrogation

paranoiaresonance
juxtaposemeaning
exploitchaos
associative word behaviour-patterns of
perception matrixs /speech:the language of
rhythm is living matter-not fixed as appears on
page bt carrying movement/motion.of mind &
of fingers
directing-pushing-reversing-pressing-curling-
squeezing this movement is what
you feel is what moves you when you read

see my face in spotlight an dead rain i am bones
dry bones an tamarind seed bleeding an brokedick surrendering
no more bush. meat. or whiteplasticjazz or ron jeremy lickin a
keyhole i give up in out down all lay down call my friend in
NYC see new orleans architecture on twisted streets an see
follow my voice on the line see where it goes

& goes tru

DE MOKO JUMBIE

is not played.he is-has become-
de moko jumbie wipes hs face wt sleeves of bluesatin-
bloodred trousers overstepping walk among the people
who are sun/wet/burning
.he lowers his panama.they put coins in a valley of straw.

de moko jumbie puts his hat back accidentally trapping
a small cloud under it is soft&cool against
his skull provides momentary relief frm the firesky -
dissolves into more sweat slides down wooden thighs
caressing knots&vowels.

de moko jumbie has climbed the citys tallest
building.the carnival roars.he is blackblack
strongbeard .swiftboned.dancing

    dancing   dancing

     *dancing*dancing
dancedance
   ing   cingdance

de moko jumbie
spits sparks where he drags hs stilts dey step out of hs
way-he is burning-needs more clouds&whiterum
-he bends-snatches an eye frm the nearest watcher-
dips it in salt dips it in snowcone syrup-sucks it-spits de
iris out.

d' sweet socalypso dat bawls bass-he bucks&sways
involuntarily-
riddim makeim wile-redeye-possession by de drum
he sing-

keep yuh stars in yuh mout!
keep yuh stars in yuh mout

he has grown wings he has swallowed trees the
crowd keep

> *dan*
> *cin*
> g dancing dancing d a n   dan
>   c i n g   cing

de moko jumbie has multiple personalities-
                              they move
                    even faster than my pen

> *returning my gaze to a framed photograph of my*
> *mothers ear i invent 2wo men see them*
> *come with afros & Cornel West suits(2wo sizes*
> *small) remove the frame from the wall*
> *replace it with one of my love.*my love

blood stirs itself-
        the fire spreads..

nude
        warm
                body
                        slipperysmooth
                                            skin
                        texture of
        pores on hip
                    inner thigh
                                        between thighs

        the wet ooze
                            that swallows
                    and i do
                            in mouthfulls

TRANSCUBIC DESCRIPTIONS

BlackShiveringDog
SquareJointsOutlinedInElectricShock
BlueDoorBehindFrontLegsLookingUp
ItsEyeWideItsEarUp
&NowBarking&NowShut-DogsTongue
WhiteBeamSlashesItsBreastSeversTheLeftLeg
FromTheBody
HeadStillUpAtInvertedBird
WithADotOfIris-NoTissue-PaintedRim
NoticeAnotherEyeAboveTheFirstBird
PatchWorkCutOutOfLeaningPinesAgainstPink
ItsTailSharp
WindBlownBranchesSentForwardItsClawMechanic
No
ItIsVulnerableItHasStemsItIsBent&Yellow

TheBirdsTrueBodyIsBlackItsHeadRedItsBeakPink
HungUpSideDownUnderAPlayingCard
WithASingleBrownHeelPrintTriangleCut
FromItsSideCenterDividesTheRoom
Blue/YellowAtTheTop-OnTheYellowBut
CastingAnInconsistentShadow-ACatYawns
WrapsItselfIsARobe-SitsAboveAHead-WhichIs
VentedStriped&DottedCrudeBlackWhiteCircles
AnArmFootAHeadKneeAWhalesTail-More
WindSweptPines-NeckIsBrownSkinEyeBrowYellow
ButThereIsGreenHereToo

MINDKEEPSFLASHINGITSUP
TOYOUTOKEEPYOURSTEADY

the regard/less of the norm-being thirst for
sunflower petals

or sumtin.

bt do people need to be told about life-
their lives.i`m not sure bt ego factors
regulate the spiral ascent of membranestates
wt apologetic handshakes

these trees are as barren as the field they swim in
it is a
DesertAntartica @ dawn–
Cypress against yellowbrown hue of African morning

bent skeleton deformity

the guard checks my ticket stamps my passport asks me
'where is your uniform'
with/out blinking i say 'its in my pocket'
–he looks–we fall-over and into my chest

my want:
to overlap&crush method
be it non or un or careful steps
over sleeping bush

BLACK&WHITE DARK SHADOWS

used to stay up to watch
𝔇ark 𝔖hadoᵗws
wt m'grandmother.1975
after 11-de ol`man snorin-
me an she on de couch me
btween she toes watchin
𝔅arnabas 𝔈ollins

white face sharp bone pointy collar
    black coat&cape stiff devil teeth-dem fangs
-double incisors that sunk
    into the flesh of de swooning neck
                behind de straight black

bt de dagger had de villain f'Barnabas
    lyin in a coffin

all light off in de house

dogbark&fridgehum she dead&gone
            me
              in dark shadows

INTERPRETATIONS

One/s strong
10thousand/stronger

am a child naked dance
on rocks
by the sea

wh?t does wh?t
havtado
wt anytin

eliminate all ?s.useless.know it
by feel tell
it by smell.ear x know it.useless
bt know it

Killaz heatseek
but many're
frozen

tonight/morning
lamplight-carpulse-havnt seen-
the moon

african robes
make zebras
of us

DEADEYE

cactushorrorpulpmilkfriction
deadeye
rabidgashslitmorewtrazorbone
deadeye
fatcrutch&walkinstickfreaksstaggertruthesleepingdaylight
deadeye
aliveheartpumpininpantyhosehanginfrmgamblersbeard
deadeye
bellhopmasturbatorsejaculateprunes&cherryblossom
speed
deadeye
realtimetrajectoryofexplicitlove
deadeye
lizardskinlipsrubbermaskedspanishpornboysipsirisjuice
tiedwttwistedmusclewhippedwtuncoiled
crownofthorns
deadeye
dogseyeinateaspoon
tightcurledbestsellingauthorbitchgrinnintearsofcoins
deadeye
arawakgingerpapayaseedrevealedhercuntwhilesheread
baudelaire
deadeye
2wofingerspullfrmnostrilsripyourfaceoff
unmaskyou

TIGERBALM

sketching dust slowmotion step across bone desert
into shapes – one which
lights the wheel
the spasm exposes the truculence of memory
pushes the cart of noises beyond
the 15eenth of everything
a cutlass falls spinningspinning falls spinning
tru the tents striped apex it
divides the now silent conversation

bu(t
win)d
moan(ing
wt)
hunger
(blows
our
eyes
o(ff

she brings us tea we exchange alibis
confuse the jury refute all sensibility
exteradicate all evidence bt our armpits
have swallowd

BENGUES BALSAMIC OINTMENT

ignites tarpaulin

fire runs burning down
running hill down burning

the river starts here

ripples cold
caress the water

rivers hair
longer than

bird wing startles morning

PLASTICINE
soundtrack: eddie you should know better/curtis mayfield

I n f l u e n c e
vs.copybooktears.swallowing.infinite.divergent.they said
i was.i opened to them.believed them believing i could
cough whole paragraphs.deconstruct every idiom i
meet.no i need Cyclops' Xmen helmet.lemme wear your
sunglasses.

i am be.coming to understand.
i am be.coming to further frm home.
i am be.coming the alien & then here-
                                        bellyfever.sudden twist of
mood)psycho/logical sport & mine.
becoming brainsick sciencefiction fuck medicine
becoming invisible.becoming water-
already drowning.caught the next train.(wind tru window is
cold an cuts my eyes bleed tears.my consolation.be it this.the
infinite vs the definite.

2 t i n g s i s d e f i n i t e
future & furious bulk of unconscious laughter.
so warm.

Nothing really is really new every we see how we see
appears in cubic sense only as
approximateappropriation/cannibalizm from another
angle)of relevancy to the direct now for example
6seconds of-HighEnergyDub.Anti-matter
propulsion.fried chicken pills.take another pill-teleport
to Havana or Aranguez savannah

relentle$$ acce$$ to information
the way things re/appear is what new eyes see–a case of
the egg before the egg or death after life or

u n w r i t t e n t e x t
which is it an it an an is it an is is it the time it takes to
go around or go tru

a subtle timewarp might accompany the latter

The Flambeau

this part of the journey takes place frm inside a
flambeau
this is your ship your mode of transport
which brings us back to paraffin
The Flambeau
is made by filling a beer bottle with kerosene
wick is twisted flammables-cotton-newsprint fixd into
bottleneck
do not shake
this
carry you
tru bush an all kinda nigga sweat
into hills dis time tho'-you
are its fuel
by drinking the paraffin-faster than speed of thought
when lit
and faster
than being carryd overhead tru Malick Village

basic technology

light
without colour
without teeth
without form
hold out for manna

C e r t a i n   o   m i s s i o n s
are of course understandable.this and the uncut essence
conspire to provide without clauses the full effect which
when viewed tru a rainstained window in Malick you
will see the spirits of your ancestors rise and dance from
the steaming bush

and when the rain stops
 they will call you for
babash rum
call you to see how you dey
 will call you for
pacro water bois bande an'sea cockroach
 will call you for

      arawak kisses
            arawak kisses
                  arawak kisses

in a bowl of honey
in a cup of brown sugar
in a wet mint valley

2
europeisinmyass

dontsleeponyourbackyoullhavenightmareso
nethingilearndformyselffictionispretensein
theroleoftheego4wordscallouscaseouscuntb
ushwasintranceshesveryeroticashesvery6r
ejectedwordsperfectriverpeacezincalloydisa
llowretrogradeifyoukeepwritingyoullbreaki
ntearsbroccolifishtearsassociativebehaviou
rcalmisuponmebtbigbooksLacanEcritswhat
willidothereisachapterontheletterintheunco
nsciousdescriptionsthesilverplatedscissoral
mosttouchestheteacupilostitifeltitgowasyes
terdayorganisetoothacheslowbuildinguntiln
extweekwhenitwasunbearablehadtogodenti
stwtaminerslampstapledtohisforeheadwrin
kledlipsfrmcrackedresonationsmesmerised
bysundaysoverheadmachineryundulatingbl
oodstreamburningbetweenthighsmypriceth
egestureremainsintactinsectveinspeechcon
formstoslenderlimbnumberssunsunsunmy
willisburnlittlefolkorbituaryfortheimagined
deadtaffiesweet+talked+goneheadbackande
yesstraightoutfrmnewspapereyeslookingov
ercheekbonebecausetheheadisheldbackbyth
edyingmoodalwaysaseveralsotightwalkrop
eingupacrossconcretevalleyholdingthembot
hfromfallintruwindowstheheadleansthefac
edripstheheadleansthefacedripsthefacedrip
smoltensolderdropsfallsl½ow¼lystretchingt
otheceilingofa4bedrmflatthesittingrmispav
edwtshingles&agueprofanity&colicstruggle
againstawindowwindowcrashestheyfallbaw
lasdownspinning4000feetaboveeyelevelmir
rorofinfinityfrmwheretheyfallevenskyscra
perslooklikemarginalsuicidesofbonsaimeat

windows2voiceerrorsalivatheslapwokemyw
akingswiftcutrushnoisejazzhissingfromstre
etbelowalgerianmarkettruecosmopoliticalsc
eneshearniggabawlintensifylooktruthewind
owsofthe13thfloorobservebriefcasegettingo
utoftaxitaxigettingoutofmanmangettingout
ofbriefcaseshelightsanotherthenwesiplemo
nionsyrupsameshitgavemearash2wksagon
owimsickagainriddimbusdestrategytraditio
ndictatesthatimustplaymydrumtalkingdru
mdancingwordssteppintosyllhypnotichipho
pmyriddimgobusdemstrategysureigotmyhe
adontighttootightsomoreblueswontpacifym
eriddimbusdestrategywelfarecustardinabo
wlonthekitchenfloorbulletrainastormoftear
sthemorewedisagreethemorewelovewelovec
isternbitchwhippulloutofcambodiacliponba
dgeofgeneralsamhocaughtbyredflashofrust
redwounddeepyellowhalothesuneruptsitisc
oldsocoldsointhispeculiarmotivemachinefig
htforpeacelipsofexcesscrypticpulsedripflux
recapitulativeconstantclingtofactorsofhone
stlybelievemeihavenotliedsimplydisturbed
myancestorsmasagenwalked80milesbutmy
eyesarefoldingawakeandtheswinginggatesd
raggrassscreamingbehindmethestenchthat
eruptsisofburntwatchbandsastrangerstong
uefingersmypalmiinspecttheticketwttheeye
stillwarmstillbreathingDJgunmanwassuspi
ciouswingsofnobodyahingeofbonebetweenfl
ammablefluorescentorangemyskinfluoresc
entgreenhescomingrosepetalsreleasetheirs
permcactusfrondsenclosestreetfunkhotred
burnbronzefromstonefromsteelremembert

he1sttimeyousawaghostsisawanapparition
ofobanhoytewalktrubothroomsinwhitewasc
aughtlaterthatnightwtmyfingersintocoinsfr
mdeoldmansshirtpocketbehindheglassescas
ebadbodybonebuckbreezebushbeardbruiseb
lessedbebergamotbackbonedropdeanchorw
alkupdatroadcarrycarrymyshieldofcrotons
pearsjunglebelowyellowjungleiwishyouwere
heretheredibisessitoutsidemywindowthewi
ndowsgoldenframeattractsevensnakesfrmt
hejunglebelowyellowjunglewhereeverythin
gsalwaysinseasondipmytonguedownmorni
ngsforpommecythere&mammyapplethemo
mentthatismissingistherevelationofthought
myhandsshookwhenistoodtheyaretheirown
theladywhochangesthesheetsisdressedlikea
nurseherpenisextendsunderherapronbuthe
rfacesoft&warmwhenitouchedherthenthec
urltriptiptopcrawlofaniguanacomingintomy
roomgettingintobedwtmeweeatboursinbeen
heresinceseptemberitsseptemberagainconn
ectivedotsmyroomisapaintingofherebecould
youwishthoughtofrevelationisthemissingm
omentcrustaceanteaaffirmativepositionvie
wdownovercloudstrubarbwirewindowstosof
twhitecanvasahandrisesfrmtheblurcatches
thewingsinitsgripstirstheflyingmachinevo
mits29japanesetouristswttheirheadsinmac
ybagsmymentalselfmotiveisinmotionmotiv
atingchromesynchronicspuninswilltissuelu
ngfullofgrapesdestrictionstimespacetorotat
ecreateconvulsionsshiftttherealoutoffocuscl
oudsonsanddisappearunderwheretheresahi
ghwayfencedwt87moteldoorsambiguousbea

uty&eclecticmutationsplanetdreamstoostu
nkinblazetoforgettorememberwhowhatwhy
itwasgonebeforiarrivedonlyafragmentrema
insdattoodissolveslikesugarinsalivawhoisbi
llycampbellasnakeskindealerontheavenueo
ftearsaspit&shineshoehorninbriefcaseoftea
rsa2wonunchakukillerabscesspiercerjazzs
permcockburnshardfondledinmorningcolds
ocoldeventhumbtacksmoannmetabolicamp
hetamineuserwtthesunbrowntantheautoma
ticarmconcealedinherpurse1950s**austinca
mbridge**leatherstructureofboneinfingertip
protudingskintorninpulpofpusfiercemetalri
msofcentipedeinsectveinsheinsistsonlemon
greenicanntgivehermyloveisopentopersuas
ionirubthemagicpenejaculatesorangedyeshi
tshotacrossthehorizon2palmsteepleheldfir
mtoherbreastatmoaningplywoodjunctionha
llucinogenictonguetiptwistinginagonisingde
aththroesmyhandbrokeninvicegripunicornl
ipjazzsingerslipagainststereowindowdeathi
snotenoughthisshapeintowhichthedogsvoic
erepelsvisiontreewingtouchesoceanoceanw
erunindrowningunderseaarejewelsgoldbron
zebrassrimsofsilverchromeintensityahouse
crumblesinthedistanceimountmyhorsehors
esmadeofmetalsculpturefromscrapyardspo
kesformanesparkswegowetdustarmourweg
ohouseisburningburningtheyarecominghou
seisburningwegotruwindowsdonationscrapl
ightteleeyereflectingdonationhumangenom
eprojectcircular25b:fingers10ankles2elbow
s2forgottenbody90%atanygiventimenose1b
ebopbrownstreet&crosswasthealleywher

edownwasdebebopwasdatsnatdatstraned
atsdizzdatsdextergordonsspeedona¼reedhe
uses2wotonguestoplay1inbody1inheadblow
indeoriginalbawlthiscombustionproducesac
ryaJAZZwailalongkissonbrasslipstweeee
zealabamafirehumangenomeprojectcirc
ular25cbrain1mouth1tonguesmanyoneinm
outhmanyinheadblackintellectualsbuskinbr
ownsuitsguerrillawarfareisoutofprintsoimd
econstructingthesimulacramaticsituationso
fthisexistentialcollagewordbeatriddimiss
nakerubbertwistininabarrelwhowantstosw
apigotghostrider&doctorstrangefrom77luk
ecagewaspowermanin75blackpantherfrm7
6bodykisscircumferencebodydiescomeagai
nviolentpampastrapmetalsoftnesschillieye
hairineyeoptrexeyewashsoftnessdeadbody
shiverjuptoSelDuncansmarinesqjazz1949u
mptoArtDeCoteauplayinmyfunnyvalentinei
nbossanova@seamen&waterfronthall1966j
eepfunkseranadesafricansfoxtrotinyorube
ahnightdruminhillsaboveportofspainbuckn
eckcannibalismindisroomwereonthetvni
ggaschewindeyfingerboneseatingourselves
thisbloatedcorpselikesewerlakepuffdeat
hcraterfleshgrainyporouslumpskinshealso
ateherselfshowingusboldlyherviscioussig
httrulynudecomebackcomebackcomeba
ckifadeinkfingerswetpaintedirisoftruepigm
entofblackhoneyrapidlipsofmiricles&dustb
readthecityappearstobebuiltonplateauxit
isoratleasthighuphillslookout&seasee

itsover

3
hicona

or

pimpfunk ina jimmypump

1: ash in non-places

who ws that you killed someone in the subway pushed
the blade wt fear said:made me.vague.victim ws tho'in
yo'description bt when spoke i saw him falling then you
in lifecell sadness.

BlackABlackMagazine.spotlight   on   revolving
billboard-went to the ICA ws busy bt lifeless like airport
white walls.non-place/space.fake artists asking for
BlackABlackMagazine.as yet unpublished.

kneecap rims like a shield which is itself vulnerable.

eyes then in house where light pours tru paraffin.

more signs of your imminent death.

my infinite hopelessness.

2: running&can't

a soldier.out standing a prison side.gravel faced.gun wrapped around hs back in Castro-guerilla fatigues.me walkin past when he screams

RUN

and we run,back frm way i came.

looking up see a sperm-streak shot acrss sky abover us.the soldier collapses.hs face folds wt fear contortion −

PEOPLE GO DEAD!

&then.houses tumble down a hill.

the way i ran tho'.that i might die.the way i ran i ran sideways fastest.tried runnin front out bt run same ol'cant run dream sequence.

slow fade

3: she shot nixon or afraid to climb down

motherfukkers stole my book.bus ride tru dark & over
flyovers.my joans!you bastards!i had to bust.i said bust wt
dialect bush.my thirst for violence xploded in d'bedrm
bt 1st   in the chinese takeaway-a haute couture
emporium.i stole 2 cans of ice cream an'paid for
chicken-took the bus bt had to bus'dem ass-dey stole my
book an'would not bend so i had to break dem.

she.she tho'.she flexed sex swimming naked in nylon tear
pond wt snails crapaud an'a tortoise who when she saw
she screamed-hs skull was blackchrome wt a gold
sequined rim-raised it-we swam out.green water.nymphs
in less silk than buses dat night.we made it to the bedrm-
2 cans of Kentucky ice cream & my hard jazzfinger.

> apart frm the pleasure principle the rooms were raindark
> early morn or raindark & it was:sex against the window
> chaos&complexity.more rain.i got to work late that morning
> without my bag for
> got it home-my notebook!
> how could i

how.my joans:afrodisia.i want my book.ws so
violent.sittin on the bus wt the
grinnin cunts.i want my book fuck!-psychotic fist to
solar plexus-blastslap upside head-choke round de
fatneck-steelcap kick catboot in face-
i roared an bit hs hand-*i waant my book!* so
violent.muttafukka didn
even flinch.show no sign of pain so i really
tore.broomstick into neck of broken beer bottle-jagged
speartip plunging in de fukas shin-stick broke-left bottle
in bone-bt a a look at dis*!motafuka wheres my boook!*

fierce desire for my paperback-my rare joans !

AFRODISIA
old & new poems by Ted Joans

ah doh hav it

in dis limp drawl

doh hav it

muthercunt!yes! i kept jammin-chokin the cunt-raw on
d'bus head almost grounded in breakback yoga crunch
backwards bend-squeezing-choking dat cunt-till my
joans-

                              popt out.

4: garden

listening to portable jungle in a wet garden beside a
flooded river.earlier the river claimed lives-we saw it
live-there were children-crushed against a boatside
while news of the carnival spread by radio

rusty blues man McKlutchie was a tailor by day-this
evening saw him sharpening his guitar strings-he came
down to the harbour

they died screaming-until their screams died too

we thought-it mustve been McKlutchie-twisted muscle
of night-making plans to meet trinidadians in plywood
fete that night-but out all day and then she wanted
to go home - change

B   i   g   7   0   s   h   i   g   h

5: blackglassriddlepuff&70speelback
soundtrack: loves'symphony/barry white

5 letters in a book a cousin of mine visiting mt lambert
brought them he left to go to town-
i saw the deserted towers
i left.he'd be gone before i got back.i forget to take my
letters
bt then in futuristic pinkcity after the chocolate show
2 men pull woolcaps down.put their shades on over dat
then
baseballcaps.i'm walkin upstreet feels like newyork-st
marks place-continue walkin get home in time four
letters.

the missing letter

rainy7os popartdrama substantial detail.sent into the city
wt emotive speed for a package inside a package inside
the package a letter frm Kwame Toure in a volkswagen
under starynight & when they're gone we make
love/until you are gone.the image of you i could not
now re/know.see no

6: altitude/firstly,de animus
scene 1

> i am calling frm country road.interchanging conversation eludes bt basic contusion ws trees–valleys–a voice–maybe the radio.i am shown the airwaves frm inside the radio.dial rollin down the band i am told who each station does.all forms of blak muzix.

> bald DJ DeepSoul tells me a story:

scene 2
(critical paranoia)

> before we came we saw a film.really raw.blue wt pretence to simplicity bt explicit sex scenes– copulatinghorseslongcock acrss her back hs face became almos(t) human comescene reverting to actor/actress weirderotic bisnis.face&hands.

> i had to speak to the DJ i felt   .paranoid.

> > *2 miles over valley holding dem both frm falling off*
> > *ropeladder into the sun*
> > *cup of waterfall in intimate perspective of central focus while*
> > *DeepSoul flexin dubplate*

7: Snakemuscle twistin ina-luminum buckit

scene 1
soundtrack:speak for yourself/zedd

well before yu get up
                come here an'say
hello @ 1nce

doing a reading put on my boots a   jericurl dred
tells:dont lose any more hair.i go to the reading bt
                deresaband on stage playn

peopleriddim
peopleriddim-a so dem say
keep dem bad vibes away

scene 2
free soul/john klemmer

a gathering of peoples at the crossroads
2wo sides compete for the people
the first transparent the 2nd postracist-
wants to bring back slavery
he rides in on a horse- grey suit & fierceboots
draggin a sawdust&bleedin blackman in a net

weturnaway

anywayenufornow   *how bizarre*
                an'reports are still comin in

8: cedar

the rogue ws puny bt he'd managed to force himself tru d'keyhole when i came in he was suckin on a slice of sugarcane i'd left for dinner he was flylike wt horns hs body like targravel when d'light cut tru d'kitchen red ws reflected when i observd my right shoulder+head tru an unsteadycamcorder white margins focussing eye approach him.he turns mec/hani/cally like

GORGA
TERRORBEAST FROM THE SEPTIC SEAS

spits green lava at me i shift it hits d'cameraman hs leg pulps i shove d'table cutting him in half against d'fridge door handles come tru hs stomach he bucks moans like samaan tree fallin

9

we were about to have sex she had a face that had been
crying
she said she
would not be able to come
that she'd used all her water for tears

10: the buff
for my father

they believe in electricworkmen here they give them
wine the compressed, fear of the
stairway,that leads down krik
                              krak
it was about
                    computing.

5Dimensional objects appear to bulge from the hand
held screen

rain drowns the traffic,

umbrellas aswideas latrine roofs,lashing raincuffs the
knees of me,

bt albert what did i do,you told me the next time i you
how *i* felt.
an' there was tenderness there,
on that watery mountain

11: budfunk&godshots

1

drove out to the city tru the night for
friedchickengumrot
dead Tubs in budfunk spread on the wooden bridge
over the river into the village

2

¾ flares on the avenue.waiting for a taxi bt a hearse
stops
we watch the fireworks from a crease of panama beard

3

bizarre incident after bizarre incident
she ws burning i ws helpless even the father was
stranger as if in des/kies

12: carambola

frm overhead at island and we're here again chest is
fulla green country air

carambola

balisier,poui,wet bamboo,driving

shoplifters magazine.liquid danger.painfaces.
leaving de ol mans handshake f'last.
no where remembering here

shoplifters magazine spread out on barbersaloon floor

carambola

calling or in flesh indistinct

13: a diagram of an ear suspended

when i woke this morning the sun ws nt yt abrighted it was greyblowin beige smog bt now again it reflects on the poplar leaves a soft cool wind blushes creeping tru the window

they cut his legs off while i had dinner in a blushing restaurant.frm the bedroom he was moved to a small room reserved for dying.

i had been trying to stop the operation to save his leg he tho' wanted it over and cut

bulgarian farmers dodge the spiral rain

harpsicord melodrama unfolds

the purpose of life is to stay alive

a cough comes from the front room

they cut his legs off and when i came back he was resting i lost my job they fired me

14: 2wo dreadlocks

the bombsite resembled a bargainbasement bt outside
the sun lit hills lilting caressing sunday afternoon a
silkblueshirt ina (dust

      same shirt was on the news dat night dis time i
            bought it

gallstonesgrandfatha buckmouth leans over the bonnet
washing hs arms armpits & sockets)sickness water,
mumbles–

de whola-ustralia ws rucked by de capture ade 2wo rastafarians

        but what were they held for

well boy,idono
idono/cause
he no dred hada afro
rims back an skulls like starving
TVfaminehungerers drowsy
in white
on de festival
bed

15: tropiques & the carnival weekend

FRIDAY

i'm mirrorfront posinin sharpseamed english clothes.big
lumpamoney in backpocket.same room i always had bt
house is uncommonly silent.

DRIVING

down country road.car slams in sideways ditch
.old man frowns+hisses(his car)

CARNIVAL WK/END

i'm mirrorfront posin.put microtab in fub for D.
who's never had.here.i'm here where am i i'm @ this
place.

then FATLEGSONDEBED

later at the party.a giant tv screen sees i believe -
technicolour boxing or she tru soft doors of light
i'm glad to be here.glad to be there.

16: carnival

travels to & from the carnival along bending swerves
on trains hug the mountainside/on buses to the focal
point where there is food&music–a crowd gathered in
the overcast

a murder had taken place a woman the protaganist i
cannot remember who she killed but the sick of it
hung in the air by whispering threads of cobweb
sadness&joy&kaiso &the sunset slight left of the
downhill was a roti shop

returning and treated so smiles and curious eyes
of the women at the junction of above one of them
was you but we seemed stranger than even this
conscious perception she lived in a cratewood paraffin
& tungsten house i met you at the carnival we took a
long train

17: indian red

i get lost in strange city.this actors swiming pool is his bathtub in the yard.in this episode he is interviewing a blackwoman.spins on his swivell hires her.nxt scene they are in bed.all this time with a wooden map of the caribbean nailed to his back. teragaton.

a special dog and these english rites.he's never been in this special building.special building has red carpets which are exclusive to all bt beefeating upperneckers. however-they allow the dog.today.

i arrive at work and everyone wants to buy me drinks but then i go cruising and the dog interlude.the actor's my father unmasked as myself at his age.we waltz down the bellbottom streets and through hills of musk in a dim-moon valley.

i arrive at work and everyone-my boss.she's standing in the doorway.i'm ½ a day late.adrian brings me a bottle of babashbushrum-tells me where everyone is.2 round back fixin instruments

tell her i'm vrrysrry.she's very femme fatale standing in the doorway smoking a cigar and doesn't fire me.tell her this shirt in my bag is the
only shirt i have with me.today.

shirt of my favorite funk.indian red

.teragaton

18: ting
soundtrack: betty davis/70sblues

in a hot brown field in a shack with a beautyfull woman
in the field a house of drawers behind us a stadium
where from our frontdoor sunshade reflects sprinters in
grainy close up of blue thighs flashing

our ct/ao/dg is long legs wear stockings

bukka white/aberdeen mississippi blues

we run frm the horned wild boar wt the shaggy fur over
the chicken wire her white dress exploding

new location: Mitagua Junction.3am
a woman acrss the sidewalk her head against the wall
she has a jericurlafro whch bleeds a bloodstream into
the street she tells me why when i walk past the 2nd
time

behind the wall is a hospital emergency unit where the
pharmacy used to be biglights a volkswagen ambulance
the receptionist shows me

brownchildrenonotherchildrensbicycles

tells me to walk the bleeding home to Mitagua which
is a village up the hill to our left the bleeding agrees
already up and walking/holding
her head

i tell the receptionist

bukka white/pinebluff arkansas

i'd take a cab bt i'm broke till i get paid
tomorrow

we laugh she gives me 3£s

where was i coming frm the stadium an
australian desert running from beasts
the university

are you.a communist

bukka white/the panama limited

19: nigga sams bionic parts

1

cloud piercing workplace but never in office.always
out/standing .ritualistic manœuvres in the wasteland
between
cloud piercing workplaces–so barren/wide

2

she walks wt the longest legs she notices no one
completely beautyfull head wont turn left enough to
view her.
hairborn niggas punctuate the dust.

3

the police are after the guy who sold me the shoes
fugitive loose
in the wasteland between cloud piercing
workplaces.*visavista*.i can see him run
behind the wall tru the coolie garden outo the
savannah whch's 2metres deepflooded

4

look.over there.a rustred cloud piercer
people around a hole
in the ground.electric crane.they're moving
…
frm there to its here home
…
is 8 fingers tall

& the queen of caucasia can be seen from here sharing
tongues wt nigga sam

20: a guava tree
for my mother

her breasts were sore i'd seen her years before
as shouting woman behind the fence and the orange
tree across the green frm walking 2nd avenue.she was
such a modern poet then bt now she appeared to see
the doctor

i listened to dem bitch it got dark out in de shed.still
wt her & she teacupbreasts which pained her waiting.i
knew then how it would end.

the guava tree is fruitless this year i'm here.is:cut
out/down/rootburnt was my best friend in the
yard.ok.the orange tree reached the roof and the
savannah view frm hot galvanize and the avocado trees
bt you were different.

so seeing.the guava tree burndead last july and the
doctor she also dead then the screams which came
from inside the house made me realize that dat that dat
whole chapter of my life was
deadburn/burndead&ended(off.like
psychictravel silverspine gut cut
then neverness

genealogy.became ash with the burning brain
of 74yrs history ws bury/d and then 48 i cant explain
but the sadness it came.without stopping to see where
my friend had been cut&burning murder.

the bedroom doors are lockd shes waiting.with her
lump in teacup waiting to see the doctor bt.i
already know how this will end.

from the bedroom come tears & please-he wants to go
she begs him no-grinds more tears frm her eyeballs

he stands the bed creaks he stands he wears
brown.shortsleeved indiansilk sits in the cornr fixes hs
boot.there is no music here/an abcess of colour.

drab curtains/pumkin orange walls bt the old womans
ornaments in place.the laminated chest of drawers.the
dining table.the dove-brown 3piece suite- the
photographs on the wall will be turnd around. even
Ursula at 25.beautyfull bust of the princess.her
dress.appears to be sequined.it is.&pink.her eyes
permanently southwest profiled has been there since
1970

surrender
he's leaving
he is
he's leaving
he
he's leaving
he is
he's gone)

the roof heaves wt   oldwoman heaving.bleeding tears
into her anturium dress.
crying so that my heart twists helpless.the shouting
stops suddenly silent.

then she leaves
and i'm not sure
how it'll end anymore.

4
teragatonic sampling

asafetida

**surround your awareness
wt awareness for your surroundings**

exhaling   trees bent with my
blink.clouds went

                                                            down

        in new hat bt nobody notices

bandagedglasseslady bought 1 small Baileys & 1 rum

2hrs sleep cant keep my eyes open all i need is my nose
open
everything else is a luxury

there were dramastic changes-woman on ch4 pot
debate

                        well i been smoking cannabis for 40yrs-
                        Kris Krishna in the audiance

missing part of New York Storys

we took the F train to
LAFAYETTE&BROADWAY
brownsteelstairways

> **DO SPORT
> NOT DRUGS
> PAY TOLL**

deepfriedduckling&tofu *New Hung Wong House* @
212 grand
roi jones collected prose&plays
dexter gordon&memphis Queen

sittin in Times

> bitin the bride
>
> a dog walks past
>
> in tshirt&scarf

THE MUSEUM OF MODERN ART

jacob lawrence:the exodus
boccioni:unique forms of continuity in space
marcel jean:spectre of the gardenia
barnett newman:RED
andre breton:poem object
alberto giacometti:woman with her throat cut

jazz crusaders:new time shuffle

PRAYER FOR CYCLOTHYMIA

SUSPEND REASON
i walked across the room
SUBSTITUTE TIME
i'm not sure now
if i'm insane or near to
destruction.i must be.
will my nose bleed. i'm dancing. wt fire
when vice grips my skull
between cartilage&cranium
eyes waiting to burst at any moment
at any & every at once
(forgetin wot i supermarket needs frm)
(slam glassing)
(broomstick metal smashing)
(idiolectophobia)
(cyclothymia)

id.'id,(psych.)n.the sum total
of the primitive instinctive forces
in an individual subserving
the pleasure/pain principle.

BASIC REQUIREMENTS
medicine
warmth
mediation
buddah
jesus
allah
jah
bohidharma
jazz
sex
subversive poetics
intimate meditation in a hotel room
Écrits

J.O.
the writer has been living here since march.he has 8
luggage & assorted bags back to montreal
earlier i saw him frm the minicab we ran 8 flights
up.turning the key the whole lock fell out.the writer
had to prise a lever wt a screwdriver while i held
matches

the plants on the window ledge have not been
watered since may no sense of human presence besides
the writers musk.tonight after the hottest day so far
this summer.

how i could stop smoking:
if i read that smoking affects yr writing

at such moments the conscious and unconscious
conspire to provide the maximum effect

UNDIVIDED MIND

how to write

core/teragatonic substance
⇩
unconscious
⇩
conscious-for scrutiny
⇩
unconscious -for final synthesis
⇩
signal to conscious that synthesis is done
⇩
writing begins

**however
it is possible
to write directly frm center**

pure thought as opposed to first thought

coffee

after just 2 wks of writing into morning
i am already filled with such pain
ready to exhale tears

the problem of being must take precedence over that of knowledge

haiku 1

all afternoon putting out stock
wondering if i bought the right colour shoe

How to write

set clock for 6.15 write 3 pages
make cartoon demon put an X tru it.

art may seem to spring frm pain
bt perhaps this is because pain
focuses our attention on detail

images

sketch as opposed to picture

a pair stroll pass in full 40s american gothic
hs smooth
beige
sharp zoot suit straw
fedora
cigar
creased ol'plastic gangster face
bt hs eyes were f$@%@*WILD

her thin
grip
waist rollin jellyroll
ass deep
stilettos
dark sunglasss bouffantblonde
wt her metal purse

'i bought them by weight
800 lbs of books'

haiku 2

jasmine scent from chinatown teapot
mingles wt midday heat

keep your mind in hell,
and despair not-Staretz Silouan

iamblacksurrealist
Ted Joans

thought defined in the absence of all control exerted by
reason...outside all aesthetic or moral preoccupations

Yoz & the Clapham pizza incident

every friday rudy & mohammed would argue about
money tonight they started in the kitchen behind
the oven badpay every friday they would argue
tonight rudy coulda bust the glass he holding in
m'mmed face but Yoz is de badpay & bossman to
kill for shortmoney friday Rudy & Mohammed would
argue but tonight ..

97

How - not - to write

3 crossrhymed iambic pentameter quartrains
followed by an iambic pentameter couplet
as opposed to
an octave consisting of 2 quartrains with the same rhymes in envelope
fashion then a sestet employing 2 or 3 more rhymes

NOT LIKE BUT IS

morning.redsmeared filter of a womans cigarette
porcelin cowhead between lettuce green peppers
& carrots
limbless blonde mannequin torso hung frm shop
window ceiling

the evolution of pure mental representation in the
plastic arts is due to the invention of
photography.
Photographic eyeballs
graphic asshole revealers

the reptiles skin is chrome it's mouth a cool wound

ParanoiacCriticalActivity:
spontenousmethodofirration
alknowledgebaseduponthein
terpretativecriticalassociati
onofdeliriousphenomena

haiku 3
sunday morning
butchers apron on a wall

vervain with kimono

the succulent womb broken glass cas)

cading

tru waterfall of violent hair-was(

p

meat decoding telegraphic cunt

sulphuric yellow
brass jukebox jazz

iamtheinterplanetarypostman

madness

mouthfulla splinters

lungfulla grapes

better be mad than sorry

is the word long,will intended readers understand
the word is the word
necessary

meanwhile back at the bookshop

ol'sicilian spy he ask:
'where for concealed book book look like book
bt wt hole-conceal document put in library'

2 bearded bros. ask me
for books by Hitler

yellowface

awareness of the I
reflected in the mirror confused
your image wt mine

carbide

ANTHONY   JOSEPH

D i s t a n c e & D i s e n g a g e m e n t

paranoia of being is you are in this bodything
which represents you
-who is this bodything-
we cant see how we're seen is paranoia of being
the ego revealer
bt in the absence of a face or if i wore a mask
i could walk through the city naked

they race faster than caustic bush

bt they embrace rather than crush

we no longer communicate

even the hidden skin when in-the deep

sleeps in a sea of mirrors

102

**2. vertical essays on surfaces using photos of walls &
streetwise iguanas**

3. jury sees photo of victim's skull

4. freedom is freedom from the need to be free

5. you are who you pretend to be

6. perilous envy of impossible shoes & amphibious
bracelets

7. ma's new girl beats wang wins nealus milikings

8. HIDs/metal halides 400(Mhz) sodium vapour

9. new gizmo traps thieves inside your car
and kills them

10. spirit lash finds tattooed armchair wt bobtail
deception

11. zoot allures shows Zappas' gunsack

12. dry bone lucidity expressed in the caseous underlung
of bionic poets

13. hardcore nigga in erection boots swallows
burning bus f' flesh

14.SUBAQUATIC EQUILIBRIUM

Such.what ride?this interface/the first pillar of
decisive temporality-beyond the serpentine
aroma which carves a halo of smoke chambers
for dwelling-so unkind to black folk

the imagined eye sees the country's rush
reflected in the speeding windows-we go deeper
into a sea of grass in a pumpengine jitney

/extending out to brightness

in kandahar village tru the bushy hills-no one
told me there were grecian ruins here-a
sprawling metropolis of rotting stone-a
pantheon,a statue of hercules in a pool of green
water surrounded by corinthian pillars

falling tru water into darkness with africa's ease

standing on a hill overlooking the stone

1. The master may determine the kind, and degree, and time of labour to which the slave shall be subjected.
2. The master may supply the slave with such food and clothing only, both as to quantity and quality, as he may think proper or convenient.
3. The master may, at his discretion, inflict any punishment upon the person of the slave.
4. All the power of the master over his slave may be exercised not by himself in person, but by any one whom he may depute as his agent.
5. Slaves have no legal rights of property in things, real or personal;but whatever he may aquire belongs, in point of law, to their masters.
6. The slave, being a personal chattel, is at all times liable to be sold absolutely, or mortgaged or leased, at the will of his master.
7. He may also be sold by process of law for the satisfaction of the debts and bequests of a deceased master, at the suit of creditors or legatees.
8. A slave cannot be a party before a judicial tribunal, in any species of action against his master, no matter how atrocious may have been the injury received from him.
9. Slaves cannot redeem themselves, nor obtain a change of masters, though cruel treatment may have rendered such change necessary for their personal safety.
10. Slaves being objects of property, if injured by third persons, their owners may bring suit, and recover damages, for the injury.
11. Slaves can make no contract.
12. Slavery is hereditary and perpetual.

(Stroud, 1856: 12-13)

17.HOW TO BUILD A TIME MACHINE

timeflight by spacelabour/alternatives to
fuelrockets/explosion/propulsion»
25th century/   portable anti-proton
tractor/accelerator/speed of light=built
in speed of universal limits-beam laser
reflection/matter/anti-matter detonation
system-collision   of   anti-matter/anti-
matter/time slows down the faster you
move-1 millionth of a gram of anti-
matter to mars and future/ separate
magnetic metal twins wt the power of
an   exploding   star
/force of virtual con+dis connection
creates wormhole/jump into worm hole
wearing african spaceboots.

Art is a way of experiencing the artfulness of an object;
the object is not important.

VICTOR SHKLOVSKY

ACKNOWLEDGEMENTS

Thanks to: my family, Louise, Darren Lewis, James
Oscar, Nia Roberts, Adrian Owusu, Kemal Mulbocus,
Keziah Jones, everyone at 213 Piccadilly, Martin La
Borde, the Chasseau Family, Christal Tranberg, Sylvia
Gaspardo-Moro and Wilson Harris

Madan Sarup quoted in *An Introductory Guide to Post-
Structuralism and Postmodernism* Second edition, 1993,
Harvester Wheatsheaf, Prentice Hall U.K.

Author photograph by Christal Tranberg
Cover photo courtesy of author

BIOGRAPHY

Anthony Joseph was born in Trinidad and has lived in
London since 1989.
(The rest is in the text)

poisonenginepress

is a black independent imprint founded in 1994 and specialising in experimental/neo-contemporary texts.

also available:

The Spaces Between Screams
by Kemal Mulbocus

Desafinado
by Anthony Joseph

forthcoming:

Budfunk&Godshots
an anthology

Paradise Garage-fragmentations d'une memoire
by James Oscar

Blackspeedtext
by Keziah Jones